Introduction

'You know, the most noble thing about us is that desire to find out who and what we really are, and to not stop asking that question, to just go on asking it. And when I come to somebody who has found a reason not to do that any more, I've found a person who has found a damn good reason to be dead.'

Ben Okri OBE, in Third Way magazine (January/February 2003)

In these bold and insightful words the writer and poet Ben Okri identifies a fundamental aspect of both the human condition and Religious Education – asking questions and seeking answers. Syllabuses and specifications explicitly require RE to explore such 'ultimate' questions with pupils, studying perspectives and insights from a variety of world faiths and philosophies, and engaging them in seeking their own insights and lights to live by, their own answers.

Writing elsewhere, Ben Okri indicates why he thinks this aspect of education is important:

'It's not just jobs that children are being educated for; it is also, mainly, to be fulfilled human beings, people who have the tools to dispel their ignorance, their fears; and the desire to create a life worth living, a future.'

Ben Okri OBE, in Report magazine (June 2002)

This publication aims to provide teachers with a variety of active approaches and strategies through which to explore issues of life, death and beyond from a range of religious and non-religious perspectives.

The various stimulus materials and activities presented have been chosen to engage, challenge and support pupils' learning from religion, and to provide opportunities for reflection and spiritual development.

Rosemary Rivett
Editor

Contents

- **1** Introduction
- **2** Ultimate questions – classroom strategies
- **5** Living life to the full – exploring some issues
- **9** Life, death and beyond – opening up the issues
- **11** Death: an end or a beginning? – discussion starters:
  - the art of Mark Wallinger;
  - sacred texts;
  - insights from Islam;
  - thinking things through.
- **16** Life, Death and Beyond: a table of beliefs, texts and practices
- **18** Funerals – reflecting on Sikh belief and practice
- **20** The sanctity of life
- **22** Questioning the sanctity of life – Humanist, Muslim and Christian perspectives on issues surrounding birth
- **25** The sanctity of life – euthanasia
- **29** Responding to issues in medical ethics

Developing Secondary RE: Life, Death and Beyond

Ultimate Questions – classroom strategies

For the teacher
Ultimate Questions are questions which engage, intrigue and challenge most people, and may include:

- What is the purpose of (my) life?
- Where did the universe come from?
- What happens when I die?
- Does God exist?
- Why is there evil and suffering?

Answers to such questions are likely to be open-ended and theoretical, and are most often answered by beliefs. Investigating the answers and insights offered by different traditions (religious and non-religious) is a significant way of discovering what matters most to these traditions.

Exploring ultimate questions is a fundamental part of quality RE. The two activities outlined here provide ways of introducing 'ultimate questions' to lower secondary pupils.

Activities for pupils

Activity 1: The 'ultimate' challenge
This activity gives pupils an opportunity to identify for themselves criteria by which a question may be declared 'ultimate'.

Provide each pair with a copy of the 'board' on page 3 (photocopied to A3 size) and the nine question cards below.

Pupils aim to identify the questions they believe fit the three categories on the board – for example, 'What is the capital of France?' may be identified as 'Answer known to me'. Expect variations, insist on reasons being given in the follow-up discussion, and encourage respectful listening to others' opinions.

Activity 2: Reflecting and responding (page 4)
This activity moves pupils from identifying ultimate questions, to identifying and reflecting on their own questions, answers and truth claims.

What is the purpose of my life?	What causes war?	Why is there evil and suffering?
What is the capital of France?	What is the speed of light?	What is colour?
What happens when I die?	Who wrote Harry Potter?	Does God exist?

© RE Today Services 2003. Permission is granted to photocopy the cards on this page for use in classroom activities, in schools which have purchased this publication.

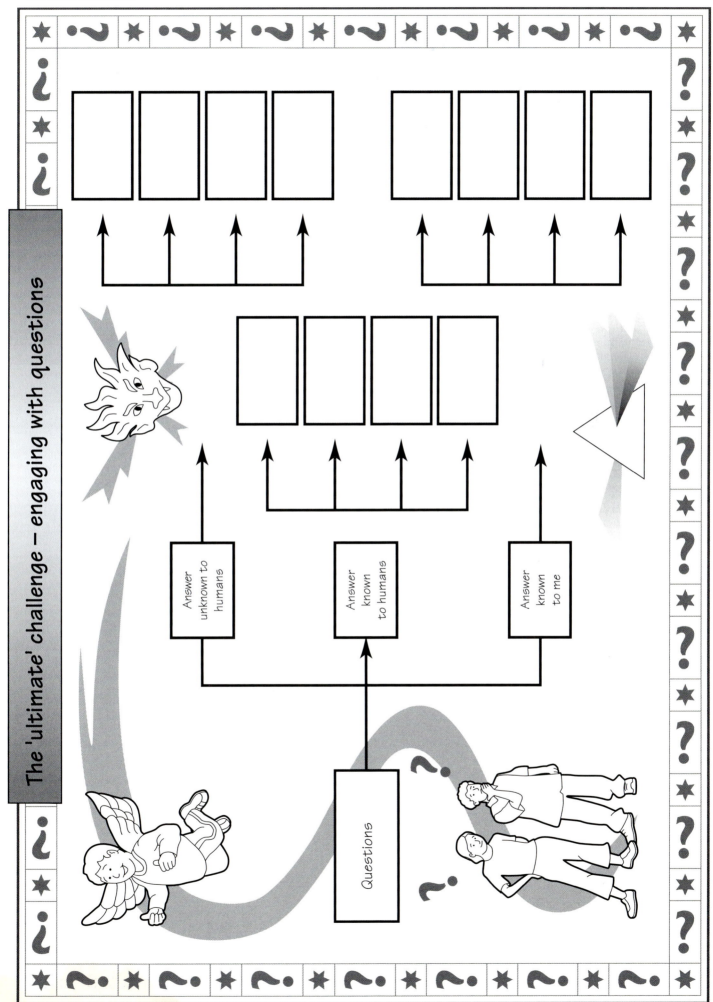

Developing Secondary RE: Life, Death and Beyond

Exploring ultimate questions – reflecting and responding

Theology

When she was five, Vera Navratil looked up into the night sky of Montevideo and asked her mother, 'Do the dead go to heaven?'

'Yes.'

'And when God dies, what heaven does he go to? Does he go to a special heaven higher up?'

On the same night in Ribero Preto, many leagues north of Montevideo, Marcos Awad, who was the same age as Vera, was looking at those very same stars. Marcos asked his mother, 'Who made us?'

'We were made by God.'

'And God?'

'And God what?'

'Who made him?'

'Nobody made God. God made himself.'

'But what about his back? How did God manage to make his back?'

By **Eduardo Galeano**, translated by Mark Fried, © Eduardo Galeano, reproduced by kind permission of the author.

Eduardo Galeano (1940–) writes and speaks regularly about the social injustices he sees in Latin American society.

'I write only when I feel the need to write … it is a celebration of life, which is so beautifully horrible and horribly beautiful.'

'I am a writer trying to get inside the mysteries of life and the secrets of society, the hidden zones, the obscured zones – because reality is masked.'

'What I like best is telling stories. I feel I'm a storyteller… I listen to voices and transform them through the creative act into a story, an essay, a poem, a novel. I try to combine genres to go beyond the standard divisions and convey a complete message.'

Activities for pupils

Read the passage above by Eduardo Galeano, then complete the following:

a **Identify** as many potentially 'ultimate' questions as you can in the passage. **How** did you decide?

b **Either**:
  i **Imagine** Vera and Marcos are now the same age as you, looking up at the same night sky. What might their questions be? How might an adult respond? **Compose** the dialogue.

  or:

  ii **Imagine** it is you looking up at the night sky, with a parent or other adult. What would be your questions? How might the adult respond? **Compose** the dialogue.

Extension work

Suggest what Eduardo Galeano might mean when he says (see quotations on right) that life is 'so beautifully horrible and horribly beautiful'. **Present** your thoughts in prose (maximum 200 words), poetry or images (e.g. a poster, collage or sequence of web pages).

Developing Secondary RE: Life, Death and Beyond

Living life to the full – exploring some issues

For the teacher

In the introduction, Ben Okri was quoted as saying, 'It's not just jobs that children are being educated for; it is also, mainly, to be fulfilled human beings.' The two activities outlined here provide ways of exploring this with pupils. Teachers may find the resources below helpful.

Books
Codes for Living, ed. Joyce Mackley (RE Today Services, *Developing RE* series)

Websites
The Clear Vision Trust (Buddhism)
www.clear-vision.org

RE Jesus (Christianity)
A useful source of personal 'encounters'.
http://rejesus.co.uk

Video
BBC *Curriculum Bites* RE (2003)
This extensive collection (2 hours) of video materials to support RE for 11–14-year-olds is useful here – see the strand **'60-Second Sermons'**.

Activities for pupils

1 **'To die for…'** (pages 5–7)
This 'card game' is designed to help pupils **think about** and **evaluate** what makes for a happy or fulfilled life. There are no 'right answers', but through **discussion** during and after the activity, pupils are encouraged to **identify** and **justify** their chosen priorities in life, and to **listen to** and **consider** those of others.
The game board is most effective if photocopied to A4 size and laminated.

2 **Case Study – a Buddhist perspective** (page 8)
Having played the game, it is useful to ground the activity by focusing on what a real person has to say about journeying to find, and living out, the 'good life'. **Catherine Hopper's story** will provide a rich stimulus to further work and reflection.

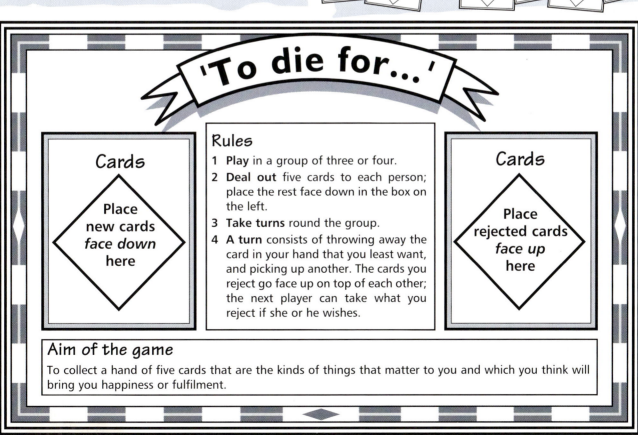

© RE Today Services 2003. Permission is granted to photocopy the game on this page for use in classroom activities, in schools which have purchased this publication.

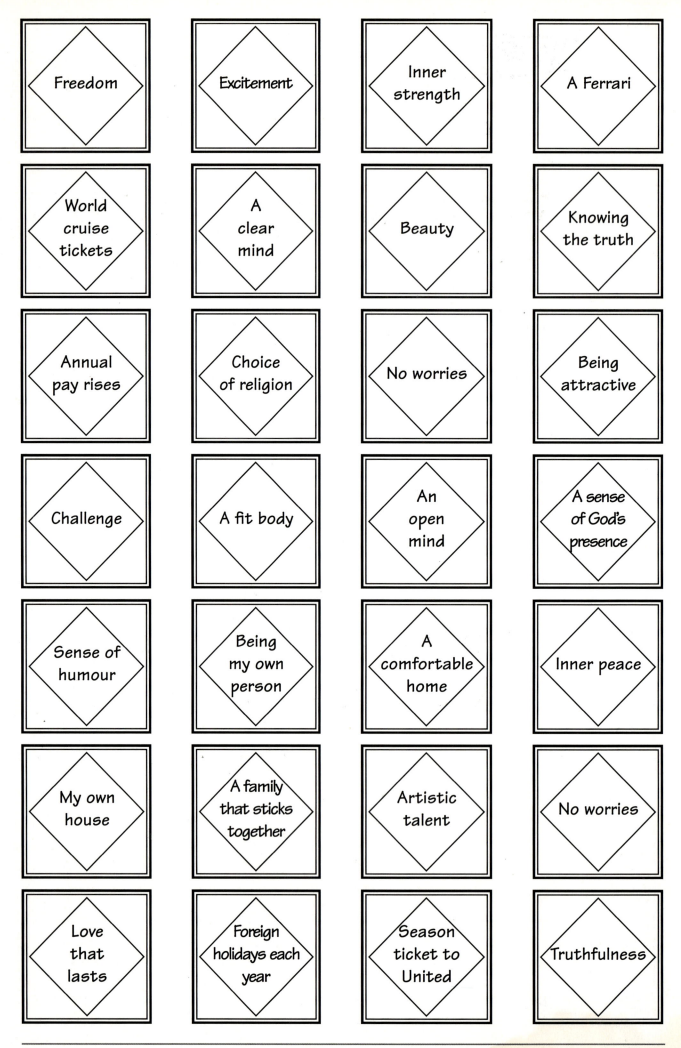

Developing Secondary RE: Life, Death and Beyond

Living a full life – a Buddhist perspective

Catherine Hopper

I came to work at the Clear Vision Trust 5 years ago. Before this I worked freelance. One of my jobs was working in the Education Department at the Tate Gallery, London, taking school parties round. This was a lifestyle that gave me a great deal of freedom and flexibility, but it didn't provide job security or a clear direction; I often felt confused by the sheer variety of interesting work I had.

I became a Buddhist in 1993. As I started to meditate I began to see more clearly what was important to me. I ended up working just at the Tate. This was a very good way for me to live out my growing Buddhist commitment. I was learning to be aware – to be mindful. I was working in a beautiful building, helping people learn how to 'see', how to notice things.

After about 9 years I was very good at this, but I knew that I couldn't do it any better and it wouldn't get any more interesting. At this point I was asked by the Clear Vision Trust to produce materials about Buddhism for schools. I am currently in charge of Education Services.

Now I've got 'sangha' – spiritual community. My whole day is spent in the company of other Buddhists, all dedicated to living out the Five Precepts. We do business in a Buddhist way: answering the phone in a kindly and attentive manner; pricing our goods truthfully at £9 rather than £8.99, and so on. We often start our day reciting the Precepts in front of the office shrine.

I wasn't fantastically well-paid before, but then I could do what I liked, when I liked. I could work or have a day off, it was my choice. Now I work a 9–5 day, which at first I found restrictive. Now I see its value. I've learned the value of commitment and responsibility, and I can develop personal friendships with the people I work with more easily than when I was freelance.

Here we are paid what we need to enable us to live a dignified but simple life whilst we work here, rather than a fixed wage or salary. We give what we can in time and skills, and ask for what we need. So we receive rent or mortgage, and a basic living allowance.

Activity for pupils (pairs)

Read Catherine's description and then:

a **Identify** three questions you would like to ask Catherine. How do you think she might answer?

b **Imagine** Catherine played the game 'To die for…'
Which five cards would she hope to end up with:
i **before** she became a Buddhist;
ii **now**, as a Buddhist?
In what ways might her choices be similar or different to your own? How might you explain this?

c **Discuss** the quotation below – what does it mean?

> Water dripping ceaselessly
> Will fill the four seas.
> Specks of dust not wiped away
> Will become the five mountains.
> *Wang Ming*

i **Suggest** the ways in which Catherine might feel she is living out this teaching.

ii **Describe** the effect on your school if everyone followed this philosophy. (250 words)

Developing Secondary RE: Life, Death and Beyond

Life, death and beyond – opening up the issues

For the teacher
Discussion of 'near death' or 'out of body' experiences is something likely to get most teenagers **interested** and **participating**.

Discussion of such experiences, backed with information and a range of responses, can be used to **stimulate** pupils to **reflect** on and **express** their own ideas about the possibility of a life beyond and **speculate** what form such a life might take.

This would provide a **starting point** for exploring what faith traditions have to say about life after death and for encouraging pupils to reflect on their own thinking in light of these.

Near-death experiences

What are they?
These are unusual experiences reported by some people who have been revived after being deemed clinically brain dead.

What sort of experiences?
These patients report a vivid memory of what happened to them whilst they were unconscious. Experiences typically include:
- out-of-body experience – 'hovering above';
- moving through a tunnel;
- golden light ;
- blissful feelings;
- observation of a celestial landscape;
- meeting others – sometimes those who have died, sometimes 'sacred beings';
- having a sense of understanding everything;
- life review;
- reaching a boundary – a cliff, fence, something that can't be crossed if one is to return to life;
- returning to the body.

How are these experiences interpreted?
For some these...
- **provide** 'scientific' proof of life after death in a literal sense.
- **suggest** that some aspect of human consciousness is independent of the body and can survive physical death.

Others say...
- **they can be explained** as false memories, or caused by lack of oxygen to the brain or misfiring neurons in a dying brain, or caused by hallucinations.
- **it is a mistake** to imagine that research into near-death experiences can ever prove that there is life after death or that God exists – these are matters of belief.

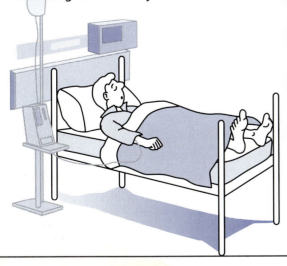

Developing Secondary RE: Life, Death and Beyond

Getting pupils thinking and talking

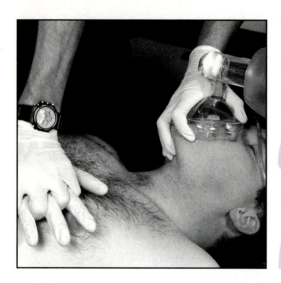

Case study

'I have had a near-death experience. I was badly hurt in a road accident, and was taken to hospital, presumed dead. But after about four minutes, the doctors found signs of life, and I was successfully resuscitated. While I was so close to death, in my mind I saw a tunnel of light leading to a gateway, which I just seemed to know was God's heavenly entrance. As I moved up the tunnel, definitely feeling full of a kind of excited peacefulness, I was turned back by a spiritual angel to live on earth for longer. I wasn't a religious person before this, but I have become interested in the spiritual possibility of life beyond the grave.'

Activities for pupils

➔ **Mind-map** ideas or questions they associate with 'death' or 'life after death'

➔ **Read** and **compare** accounts of near-death experiences. **Try** www.bbc.co.uk/religion (search for near-death experience under 'Results for all BBC').

➔ **In pairs discuss** near-death experiences – ask pupils to **identify**:
  • a **question** these experiences raise;
  • **ways** in which people might find accounts of these experiences reassuring.

➔ **Copy and cut up** the viewpoints from teenagers below. Ask pupils to **sort** these into three groups – statements they agree with, disagree with and are not sure about, and be ready to **explain** why. Use the blank to add their own comment. Feed back and discuss.

	I find these near-death experiences reassuring...	I don't think about after death because it scares me a little. I hope there is an afterlife.	I don't think that there is an end to life, death is just a new beginning.	When you're dead you're dead!
Death and afterlife is something I don't think any of us is meant to understand until we are actually dead.	I don't think I know what exactly happens, but I'm 99% sure that death is not the end of existence.	Death is the end ... of life as we know it ... but this can not be all there is; if it is, then what's the point?	There is no proof so I have an open mind about life after death.	I agree with the person who said science can't prove there is an afterlife – it's a matter of what you believe.

© RE Today Services 2003. Permission is granted to photocopy the cards on this page for use in classroom activities, in schools which have purchased this publication.

Developing Secondary RE: Life, Death and Beyond

Death: an end or a beginning? – discussion starters

For the teacher

The four activities in this section aim to provide a variety of access points into what, for some, is a difficult, sensitive, yet crucial aspect of RE.

Activity 1 Video installation (page 12)
Mark Wallinger's work presents detached observation and implicit references to Christian belief to stimulate discussion.

Activity 2 Sacred texts (page 13)
Sacred texts offer a rich source of insight into religious belief about life, death and beyond. This activity reflects on Hindu perspectives.

Activity 3 Angels (page 14)
Belief in angels is one of the main articles of faith (*iman*) in Islam. This activity provides a stimulus to explore what the Qur'an, Hadiths and Muslim tradition say about angels to illustrate key Muslim beliefs about life, death and beyond.

Activity 4 Beliefs about life after death (page 15)
Expressing the process of thinking diagrammatically is an excellent way to clarify thinking about beliefs and stimulate informed discussion.

a **Provide** pupils with a copy of the chart. Ask them to **identify** their own current belief, and **compose** a 200-word statement in support.

b **Provide** pupils with a blank template and ask them to **create** their own.

See also...
Websites
Mark Wallinger
www.artcyclopedia.com/artists/wallinger_mark.html

Ishwar – searchable sacred texts from ten faiths
www.ishwar.com

Bible Gateway
http://bible.gospelcom.net/bible?

Church of England (Christianity)
http://cofe.epinet.co.uk

Angels in Islam
www.islamia.com

Catholic Online – Saints and Angels (Christianity)
www.catholic.org/saints

I believe in reincarnation and believe that where you end up and what as depends on whether you have built up good or bad 'karma' during your life.
Buddhist male, aged 13 years

I think that when you die your body stays on Earth and your spirit or soul goes up to heaven to be with God and all those that have died.
Christian male, aged 11 years

My thoughts about death are that when you die you are born again. If in your past life you did something really nice then you are born as a human being, otherwise as an animal or insect.
Hindu female, aged 14 years

We've got to have some belief that when we die something survives or else life would be pointless. What does survive is people's memories of the person who has died.
Jewish male, aged 16 years

When we die there is punishment and reward in the next life. If we did something good we go to heaven and if we were bad we go to hell. We also get punished, or rewarded, in our grave.
Muslim female, aged 13 years

My thoughts are as soon as you die you go to heaven. Your soul goes up and is put in another body, so I think you never die.
Sikh male, aged 12 years

Developing Secondary RE: Life, Death and Beyond

Death: an end or a beginning – reflecting on the last things

'Threshold to the Kingdom' by Mark Wallinger (1959–) is an 11-minute video installation. The artist placed a video camera (unseen) in the arrivals hall of a busy UK airport. The passengers, tired from their travels, spill out through the automatic double doors and are shown displaying a variety of emotions, some relieved, some happy to be reunited with loved ones. A bored security guard stands by the door. The currency counter is reflected in the glass doors, out of which people come, but never enter. The film, projected in slow motion, is accompanied by the choral music of Allegri's *Miserere Mei* (a plea for redemption through the words of Psalm 51).

The artist says...

'I'm not interested in art that is didactic. I like it to be a bit slippery, to present a paradox … to be ambiguous…'

The critics say...

'It is characteristic of Wallinger that he is interested both in the everyday ... and in first and last things.'

'Wallinger's piece contains implicit references to the entry into heaven, with Saint Peter represented here by a bored security guard.'

'They have cleared customs, they've been saved. This banal space has been turned into heaven.'

'He's looking at religion with the same curiosity and detachment he brought to earlier works on football, nationalism, the royal family, horse breeding and racing.'

'Wallinger questions ideas of faith ... with great cynicism and flair. His interest in God really does make you wonder why the subject, 'God', is so important.'

Activities for pupils

→ **Read** the description of 'Threshold to the Kingdom'. Then read the words of **Psalm 51** and/or listen to the music of **Allegri's *Miserere Mei***. How does this make you feel?

→ **Read** what the critics say. What questions is Mark Wallinger asking you to think about? What answers do you have?

→ **Imagine** that you are the security guard, deciding who shall pass through (into heaven?) and who shall be turned away. **Decide** the criteria you would use. **Reflect** on how you would feel at having this power. **Share** your ideas with a partner and then with the class.

→ **Mark Wallinger did not set out** to reflect Christian teaching on the last things. **To what extent** might a Christian agree or disagree with his presentation?

© RE Today Services 2003. Permission is granted to photocopy this page for use in classroom activities, in schools which have purchased this publication.

Death: an end or a beginning – insights from sacred texts

Worn out garments are shed by the body,
Worn out bodies are shed by the dweller,
Within the body new bodies are donned by the dweller, like garments.

*Bhagavad Gita 2.22 –
words spoken at Hindu funeral services*

A vision of the spiritual world beyond death
Where people of goodwill and good deeds rejoice, their bodies now made free from all disease, their limbs made whole from lameness or defect. In that heaven may we behold our parents and our sons!

Atharva Veda 6.120.3

As a caterpillar, having reached the end of a blade of grass, takes hold of another blade and draws itself to it, so the Self, having left behind a body unconscious, takes hold of another body and draws it to himself.

Brihadaranyaka Upanishad 4.3.34f

As a goldsmith, taking an old gold ornament, moulds it into another, newer and more beautiful, so the Self, having given up the body and left it unconscious, takes on a new and better form, either that of the Fathers, or that of the Celestial Singers, or that of the gods, or that of other beings, heavenly and earthly.

Brihadaranyaka Upanishad 4.3.34f

Activities for pupils

The 'pictures' painted in the texts above illustrate what Hindus believe about life, death and beyond.

➔ **With a partner**, talk about what you think each means. You could record your ideas as a series of spray diagrams.

➔ What would you compare death to? **On your own**, draw your own image or write your own description. 'For me death is like...'

Developing Secondary RE: Life, Death and Beyond

Death: an end or a beginning – insights from Islam

Activities for pupils

Read the descriptions below of the role of some angels in Islam taken from the Qur'an, *Hadiths* and Muslim tradition. What can you learn of Muslim belief about:

- Allah?
- death?
- judgement?
- the soul?

Israfil – Angel of the Day of Judgement

Israfil has twelve wings, one of which is in the east and the other in the west. From the soles of his feet to his head, Israfil has hairs and tongues over which veils are stretched. He glorifies Allah with each tongue in a thousand languages. The Throne rests upon his shoulders, yet he shrinks because of Allah's greatness. Each day and night Israfil looks towards hell. He approaches without being seen and weeps. The trumpet he will blow on the Last Day contains honeycomb-like dwellings where the souls of the dead rest.

Mika'il (Michael) – The Angel who guards the Gates of Heaven

Mika'il has hairs of saffron from his head to his feet, and wings of green topaz. On each hair he has a million faces and in each face a million eyes and a million tongues. Each tongue speaks a million languages and from each eye fall 70,000 tears. If Mika'il were to open his mouth, the heavens would fit within it like a mustard seed in the ocean.

Jibra'il (Gabriel) – The Angel who is the Messenger of Allah

Jibra'il has 1,600 wings and hair of saffron. Each day he enters the Ocean of Light 360 times. As he comes out, a million drops fall from each wing to become Angels who glorify Allah. When he appeared to the Prophet Muhammad ﷺ to reveal the Qur'an, his wings stretched from the East to the West. Between his two eyes were written the words: 'There is no god but God, and Muhammad is the Prophet of God.' This was Jibra'il's cosmic (true) form.

Azrael (Raphael) – The Angel of Death

Azrael is veiled with a million veils. His immensity is greater than the heavens, and the east and west are between his hands, like a dish on which all things have been set. He sits on a throne in the Sixth Heaven. He has four faces: one before him, one on his head, one behind him and one beneath his feet. He has four wings, and his body is covered with innumerable eyes. When one of his eyes closes, a creature dies.

Munkar and Nadir ~ The Angels who question the dead in the grave

Munkar and Nadir visit the tombs of those who have recently died to determine whether they will go to Paradise or to Hell. They ask questions regarding their religious beliefs, and also their good and evil deeds on earth. The good are shown what life will be like in Heaven. The bad are shown the torments of Hell.

Developing Secondary RE: Life, Death and Beyond

Life after death – thinking things through

What do you think happens to a human being after death?

You think that survival is impossible.
You think the survival of human consciousness beyond death is impossible.

- You think scientific understanding of the world gives a satisfactory explanation for all that is real; religious impulses are purely a psychological phenomenon.

  → You are close to... **Atheist belief**

- You think that while a scientific understanding of the world gives a satisfactory explanation for all that is real, it does not provide a guide for answering questions about what happens after death, a possibility to which you are open.

  → You are developing... **Your own ideas from a range of non-religious sources**

You are uncertain.
The evidence for life after death from ghosts, the paranormal and superstition impresses you more than the ideas of reincarnation and eternal life found in religions.

- You find some religious ideas more appealing and comforting than reasonable and logical, but you do not dismiss spiritual possibilities.

  → You are close to... **New Age spiritualities**

- You think that there is insufficient evidence to decide one way or the other and until such time as evidence is available you will treat all religious faith with respect while not committing yourself to any particular belief system.

  → You are close to... **Agnostic belief**

You think the human being has a life after death.
This may include a recurring, re-cycling idea of the soul into many bodies, or may refer to a 'once only' life, death and judgement.

- You think that there is one life for the individual, after which life in Heaven or Paradise with God may continue.

  → You are close to... **Christian and Muslim belief**

- You think that rebirth after death is a real possibility (rebirths don't lead on endlessly but have a blissful impersonal end called Nirvana).

  → You are close to... **Buddhist belief**

Activities for pupils

1. In each case, how should this person then live? Express your ideas in writing, with examples and making your reasons clear.
2. Develop another flowchart with the lead question: 'How do people speak of God?'

Developing Secondary RE: Life, Death and Beyond

Religion or belief system	Beliefs	Practices	Texts
Buddhism	**Death:** part of cycle of life; no 'fixed soul' or identity; new life will be influenced by the life that is ending (through **karma**). Tibetan Book of the Dead speaks of Bardo (time between this life and next, a split second or up to 49 days) where choices are made, dependent on past life and which influence future life. Emphasis of funeral service reflects belief in suffering, impermanence and transitory nature of this life. **Enlightenment** can be achieved by some in this life (for example the Buddha) but for most means ending cycle of rebirths and entering into **Nirvana** (an indescribable state, cessation of all selfishness and desire).	**Cremation.** Practices differ between countries and branches of Buddhism. Appropriate **scriptures** often read to the dying person, to remind them of the Buddha's teachings and calm their mind. Body usually washed and then cremated; if an influential teacher dies sometimes remains preserved and stupa built which can become a place of pilgrimage for followers. Monks chant from scriptures and family and friends give **alms** (often in the form of food or candles to monks). **Remembrance** ceremonies held after 7 days, 3 months, then annually (transfer of merit to the dead person).	Desire is a chain, shackled to the world, and it is a difficult one to break. But once that is done, there is no more greed and no more longing; the stream has been cut off and there are no more chains. (**Sutta Nipata 948**) Rooted in Nirvana, the holy life is lived. Nirvana is its goal, Nirvana is its end. (**Samyutta Nikaya 3.188**)
Christianity	**Death:** end of physical body; soul continues after death (eternal life). **Heaven:** place of peace and joy in the presence of God. **Hell:** place of separation from God (suffering). **Purgatory:** Roman Catholic belief; place for those not ready for heaven where they can be further cleansed of their sins. **Resurrection:** on the 'last day' the dead will be raised, including the physical body, in a 'new state'. Jesus' death brings forgiveness and salvation to those who are 'born again'. His resurrection brings hope of **eternal life**.	**Burial or cremation.** Differences between denominations. Ceremony likely to include **Bible reading, prayers, hymns, short sermon** and **eulogy** (in praise of life of the dead person). Emphasis on hope of **eternal life.** In most denominations service led by priest or minister although in some, lay people lead. Differences in practice of **praying for dead** (Roman Catholics and some Anglicans do, many Protestants don't). **Gravestones** or plaques remembering person erected. Some visit grave on anniversary of death. Some churches read out names from book of remembrance on Sunday closest to anniversary of death.	For God so loved the world that he gave his only Son, that whoever believes in him should not perish but have eternal life. (**John 3:16**) …it is appointed for men to die once, and after that comes judgement… (**Hebrews 9:27**)
Hinduism	**Ultimate force** (Brahman) is in everything; in individuals this is identified as **atman** (for some same as Brahman, for others distinct). Atman continues after death when either it achieves **moksha** (liberation) and is absorbed into Brahman or it is re-housed in another body. **Samsara:** cycle of birth, death, rebirth. **Karma** determines outcome. Belief that if a person dies in Vananasi (Banares) on banks of river Ganges, they will not be reborn; some approaching death make a last pilgrimage hoping to die there.	**Cremation. India:** cremations take place as soon as possible after death and out of doors. Relatives prepare the pyre and perform rituals. **Britain:** family goes to the crematorium. **Body washed** and men (though often not women) dress in white. Body placed with feet facing south (towards realm of Yama – god of death). Pyre lit from north end. **Ashes dispersed in water**, often in the Ganges. Ten days of deep mourning. Each year during month of Bhrapada (September/October) families offer prayers for dead relatives.	From the unreal lead me to the Real. From darkness lead me to light. From death lead me to immortality. (**Brihadaranyaka Upanishad 1.3.28**) Brahman is the end of the journey. Brahman is the supreme goal. (**Katha Upanishad 1.3.11**)
Islam	**Death:** part of the will of Allah, a natural part of life. **Person:** a unique creation; physical (body) and spiritual (soul) with freedom of choice to live in submission to Allah or not. Trust in Allah the Merciful and in His goodness. **Resurrection** of body and eternal life after death are fundamental beliefs. Belief and actions in this life are important for the outcome of **Day of Judgement: heaven** (complete contentment, rejoicing and reward) or **hell** (separation and torment through rejecting Allah).	**Burial.** Dying person will try to recite Shahadah. Relatives and friends read from **Qur'an** and say **prayers** asking Allah to be merciful to dying person's soul. After death: **body washed** in scented water; dressed in **white robes** (often brought back from pilgrimage to Makkah); **face left uncovered**. All are dressed alike. Imam or family member leads funeral **prayers**; Allah asked to forgive dead person's sins. Traditionally **only men** attend funeral ceremony. Body buried, in contact with the earth (no coffins in Muslim countries). Body laid on right side **facing Makkah**. Believed two angels come to take charge of person's soul until judgement day.	Every soul must taste death, and We try you with evil and with good, for ordeal. And unto Us you will be returned. (**Qur'an 21.35**) Those who have faith and do right are the best of creatures. Their reward is with Allah: Gardens of Eternity … they will dwell therein. (**Qur'an 98.7–8**)

Developing Secondary RE: Life, Death and Beyond

Judaism

Death: the end of the physical body; the person's spirit continues, living on with God, who is the Redeemer and Lord. Cemetery called *bet ha hayyim* (house of life) or *bet olam* (house of eternity), a reflection of Jewish belief about life after death. Common greeting for recently bereaved (I wish you long life) does not deny grief but asserts that **life goes on in this world and the next**. Prospect of death not to be feared. God will conquer death; there is an after-life (in individual and communal sense). Fundamental belief: sum total of deeds and thoughts live on; live now and forever in ways that God intends.

Burial. *Chevra kadisha* responsible for burial arrangements. Dying person will hope to say last prayer (asking for forgiveness and share of life to come). After death: eyes and mouth closed by near relative; **body washed** and wrapped in **white shroud** (and if man, probably his tallit). Burial and brief service usually within 24 hours. Mourners fill grave with earth. **Four stages of mourning** laid out which lasts until end of 11th month following death. Memorial, tombstone or stone slab covering grave; often special ceremony. On anniversary of death close relatives recite the kaddish prayer and light candle in memory. **Periodic visits to grave** made; a small stone left as mark of visit and reminder of own mortality.

The body is the sheath of the soul. **(Talmud, Sanhedrin 108a)**

This world is like a vestibule before the World to Come; prepare yourself in the vestibule that you may enter the hall. **(Mishnah Bot 4:21)**

The dust returns to the earth as it was, and the spirit returns to God who gave it. **(Ecclesiastes 12:7)**

Sikhism

Birth and death: under will of God (Hukami Howan Ji). Cycle of births, deaths and rebirths, determined by actions in past life (**karma**). Human birth gives best opportunity for release (**moksha**). God and soul of individual are the same but distinct. Separation from God: bondage. Union with God: eternal bliss.

Cremation. Soon after death, body is washed and dressed in five Ks (if initiated Sikh). Family encouraged to mourn but remain calm and trust in God. **Sukhmani** (shabad on peace) often said. After cremation **Guru Granth Sahib Ji** read (in home or gurdwara). This 7- or 10-day reading marks end of official mourning. **Ashes** immersed in running water. Erection of **monuments** in memory of dead and prayers for dead forbidden.

All from one clay are made; in all one Light shines. One breath pervades all ... Know, the Self is not perishable. **(Guru Granth Sahib Ji p188)**

Engrossed in devotion to the Eternal; their transmigration is ended; their light is merged into the light of the infinite. **(Guru Granth Sahib Ji p1009)**

Humanism

This life and this life only. Humanists are either atheist or agnostic. They do not believe that a person has a soul which continues after death. This life is all we have and is not a 'dress rehearsal' for some future life, therefore to humanists this life and living a **good life** is what matters most. Humanists see human potential as being far greater than current achievement; each individual can make a contribution to a better life for all. Improving the quality of life and respect for personal autonomy are very important.

Burial or cremation. Non-religious ceremonies have been developed (see *Funerals without God*, Jane Wynne Willson, British Humanist Association). Emphasis on **celebrating** the life of the deceased. Family or friends often share **memories** of dead person. Emphasis on human achievement and potential as shown in life of the deceased.

Humanists do not recognise the authority of any sacred text but rather draw on a range of philosophical and ethical thinkers to support their beliefs.

Be sure then that you have nothing to fear in death. Someone who no longer exists cannot suffer, or differ in any way from someone who has never been born. **(Lucretius, c95–55BCE)**

For the teacher

These pages give basic notes on beliefs and practices about death and life after death. They can be used in a variety of ways, including:

- as a **reference point**;
- in a **group sorting activity** (for example, matching text to religion or belief system);
- **groups** could focus on a single 'strand' from the chart and research it further to make a presentation to the rest of the class;
- **pairs** could be asked to use the chart to devise twenty questions which could be answered from it;
- **individuals** could write 150–200 words focusing on the religion or belief system that most closely reflects or is most distant from their own beliefs.

Developing Secondary RE: Life, Death and Beyond

Funerals – reflecting on Sikh belief and practice

For the teacher

→ What happens at a funeral service?

→ Why is a funeral important and how is this shown?

→ Why are most funeral services in the UK 'religious'?

→ What beliefs are reflected in the service?

→ How do people cope? How might I cope?

These pages provide an activity to engage pupils in opening up what, for many, is a sensitive topic. It can be adapted to cover other religions, and thus be a useful focus for identifying similarity and difference of belief and practice. The activity complements QCA non-statutory unit 9A 'Rites of Passage'.

Pupils work with a partner to complete the chart. They identify their own questions in an environment where the RE learning objectives can be met, alongside opportunity for reflection on their own beliefs and experience.

© Ann Christine Eek/Samfoto

The cycle of birth and death in this world is ended for those who have this faith in their hearts.
Guru Granth Sahib Ji 1402:539

Bhupinder Singh

Bhupinder Singh died in hospital as a result of a car accident. He had a wife and two adult sons.

At the undertaker's, Bhupinder's body was **washed** according to custom. He was dressed in **new clothes**, including the **Five Ks**, and placed in the coffin.

On the day of the funeral, the coffin was taken to the family home where prayers were said for Bhupinder's soul. Many friends and relatives visited the house to see the body and to pray.

The coffin was then taken to the **gurdwara**, where again people paid their respects. The coffin was finally closed, floral tributes were placed on top and it was taken by hearse to the crematorium.

At the crematorium the mourners followed the coffin into the building for the short service. The service consisted of the recitation of a prayer known as the ***Kirtan Sohila***, an evening prayer generally used at the end of each day.

Everyone quietly left the crematorium and returned to the gurdwara. Here they listened to readings from the **Guru Granth Sahib Ji** and recited **prayers**. The service ended with the prayer known as the ***Ardas***, which seeks blessing for the departed.

Everyone shared in ***Karah Parshad***, a reminder on this occasion that the normal activities of life must go on even though a much-loved member of the family had died.

A copy of the **Guru Granth Sahib Ji** was placed in a room of Bhupinder's house, and for the **ten days** following the funeral it was read from beginning to end by a succession of readers (***Sadharan Path***). During this time, many friends visited the family, to listen to the reading and offer their sympathy and support.

Bhupinder's ashes would eventually be returned to the Punjab for scattering on running water, according to family custom. There would be no gravestone or memorial.

REtoday Services

Developing Secondary RE: Life, Death and Beyond

For discussion and follow-up

→ **Identify** three questions which you would like to ask a Sikh about their attitude to life, death and beyond.

→ **Find out** about the funeral service of another religion – what similarities and differences are there? Why is this?

Your task

→ **Read** the account of Bhupinder's funeral.

→ **Find** two examples of each of the four aspects of a funeral shown here, and add them to the chart.

Bhupinder's funeral

- ...opportunity to mark the soul's journey
- ...opportunity to dispose of the body
- ...opportunity to remember and celebrate his life
- ...opportunity for all to mourn

'I believe that when you die you go into a place where it is paradise for you, and you join up with the rest of your family who have died.'
Sikh female, aged 13 years

'My thoughts are as soon as you die you go to heaven. Your soul is put in another body so I think you never die.'
Sikh male, aged 12 years

© RE Today Services 2003. Permission is granted to photocopy this page for use in classroom activities, in schools which have purchased this publication.

The sanctity of life

For the teacher: Why do abortion and euthanasia in RE?

Teachers can sometimes forget how surprising it is that abortion should be the most popular topic in RE, with euthanasia and cloning high on the list too. Studying abortion or euthanasia is 'relevant' in a personal sense to very few pupils, and the danger is that these become 'issues at a distance' used by teachers for their 'soap opera' grisly fascination and ability to attract polar opposites expressed with force.

In the pages that follow, you will find some practical activities for the classroom, aimed at 14–15-year-olds, and designed to make them think more deeply about how **abortion, euthanasia, cloning** and **other ethical issues around birth and death** really turn on the big questions.

Good teaching about birth and death issues includes:

- **using** accurate and up-to-date data;
- **focusing** on the belief and value questions which lie beyond the mere statistics and the details of the law and its history;
- **using** case studies to examine perspectives and interpretations about the source of human life (God?) and the value of human life (sacred?);
- **raising** questions about emotive tactics and selective use of evidence by all 'sides' in the debate;
- **examining** the responsible use of sources of tradition (for example Bible, Qur'an, rationality);
- **offering** opportunities for critical engagement with (for example) pro-choice and pro-life organisations;
- **using** the resources of different faiths and of agnosticism or atheism to provoke better learning;
- **introducing** and using at a simple level the terminology of ethical theory;
- **asking** pupils questions about their own beliefs and values in challenging moral terms.

Big questions

Questions of origins:
Where do we come from?

Questions of meaning:
What does it mean to be human?

Questions of purpose:
What is the purpose of human life, of sex, of reproduction?

Questions of value:
What makes a foetus precious? Is human life priceless?

Questions of commitment:
What are my beliefs? What action do they require?

See also...

Video

Curriculum Bites RE (BBC, 2003)
This extensive collection (2 hours) of video materials to support RE for 14–16-year-olds is a valuable resource. 'The Moral Minefield' combines drama and the format of a confrontational talk show to explore aspects of sex ethics. A teacher's resource is also available.

Websites

RE Exchange Service: http://re-xs.ucsm.ac.uk

The RS Web: www.rsweb.org.uk

BBC Religion & Ethics:
www.bbc.co.uk/religion/ethics

CD-ROM

Interactive Moral Issues (2 CD pack)
Birchfield Interactive Plc, www.birchfield.co.uk

Developing Secondary RE: Life, Death and Beyond

Handling big questions – applying ethical approaches

Activities for pupils: Five pregnant girls talking – Who's Who?

→ **Read** the five different approaches to ethics given on the right and **match** them with the statements from the five pregnant girls given below. **Discuss** your responses.

→ **Write your own** 'applied ethics' speech bubbles.
- What would the altruist say to the egotist? What would the utilitarian say to the rule-based ethicist?
- Write five speech bubbles for the five schools of thought on another topic – for example, surrogate motherhood, euthanasia or cloning would be suitable.

Who's Who?

Utilitarian Someone who believes that considering the greatest happiness for the greatest number of people shows us what is right.

Egotist Someone who believes you can decide what is right or wrong by thinking about what is good for yourself.

Altruist Someone who believes that the good of others is the best guide to what is right.

Rules-based Ethicist Someone who says that applying the rules tells you what is right or wrong (the rules might come from God, or somewhere else).

Situationist Someone who says there are no rules but love, and you can't find what's good by thinking. They ask: 'What is the most loving thing to do in this situation?

A   When I found out I was pregnant, I was very distressed. It will ruin my life, because I've got plans for my education and career that a baby would totally destroy. I can't keep it, because my plans and ambitions will all go 'down the pan'.

B   Being pregnant wasn't part of my plan, but now I feel I have to live for the child. I'm 14 weeks into the pregnancy, and to me it would be selfish to think of abortion. I have to think of what my boyfriend wants (he says he's ready to be a dad) and of what my family say (Mum's quite religious, and has always been against abortion). I'm going ahead with the pregnancy for the sake of my family and boyfriend, and the baby of course. It feels right.

C   Before I was pregnant, I could have told you three reasons why abortion was wrong quite easily. I could have given a very 'black and white' answer to any question about unborn children in an exam at school. But now I'm in the situation myself and it's much more difficult. After my first 12 weeks, I'm only sure of one thing: I want to do the most loving thing – but what is that? If I bring a baby into the world to a miserable life of poverty and without a family (my boyfriend's against it), then is that loving? Or is abortion ever loving? It isn't murder, but it is a bit like killing because the baby has potential to be human.

D   Well, if I have the baby, it will make my mum quite happy, and I guess the baby will be happy to be alive (though you can't be sure). My boyfriend will be furious – he's already threatened to leave if I don't have an abortion. For me, I can't tell. I like the idea of having a baby of my own one day, but I'm only 17, and I think in some ways it will make my life very hard and miserable. Will it make God happy? Not sure. You weigh up all the happiness, and all the unhappiness, and try to guess the best thing to do, but it isn't easy.

E   Well, I've always known and been taught that killing is wrong, and of course I agree with that. Do no murder – it's about the most universal rule you could have. I've had to think about whether abortion is killing, and if the foetus is a person. I've had 13 weeks to think about it, and I can't really see any way of explaining abortion other than as the ending of a life. That means it is a kind of murder, and I think it's wrong. So I feel I don't have a choice – I have to continue with my pregnancy, however hard it seems.

Developing Secondary RE: Life, Death and Beyond

Questioning the sanctity of life – Humanist, Muslim and Christian perspectives

For the teacher
This introductory activity provides nine statements for pupils to **discuss** and **evaluate**. Three each come from a **humanist**, a **Christian** and a **Muslim**.

Copy them onto card, cut them up and provide each pair or group of pupils with a set.

Activity for pupils
→ **Work with a partner**. The nine cards you have been given contain statements written by three humanists, three Muslims and three Christians. **Sort out** who said what.

→ **Rank** statements from 'more reasonable' to 'more unreasonable'. **Explain** your reasons to your partner and try to reach agreement.

→ **Identify** the statements which come closest to your own point of view, and **explain** your reasons to your partner.

→ **Research** one of the perspectives more deeply and compose a piece of extended writing to **express** what you discover. Your teacher will provide resources and further guidelines for this part of the activity.

I don't believe in god or gods, so I get my ideas about abortion from thinking carefully about truth and goodness. It's never easy to deal with an unwanted pregnancy, but the mother's interests should come first.	In our holy book, it says 'do not kill your children for fear of poverty'. Before our religion began, people used to bury a baby they didn't want at birth. That's barbaric, and our Prophet put a stop to it.	In our community we try to promote responsibility, forgiveness and compassion. We don't want to condemn a young and pregnant girl, but try to support her through pregnancy. An abortion can leave terrible guilt feelings behind.
In societies where our religion is the majority, there is hardly any abortion. You need a whole society to set firm laws against things like abortion, and we do this based on the idea that God has given us a law to help each other.	The abortion question just is nothing to do with god or spiritual life. You have to be practical and think about the unhappiness that can come from, for example, young teenage motherhood. The foetus can't be seen as having the same rights as the mother.	It is God who gives a child to some parents, and God is great beyond our imagination. Who are we to go against his plan and 'get rid of it' (as the abortionists say)? Having an abortion shows no submission to God at all.
Mother Teresa of Calcutta was so much against abortion that she invited any parents with an unwanted pregnancy to send her their baby child. She ended up running the biggest adoption agency in all India. That's compassion in action.	My holy book talks about God seeing everything, even the child in the womb. I know it's difficult to ban abortion, but I can't think it's right to throw away the potential of a new God-given life.	This is our message about abortion: be reasonable. Life is valuable, but a foetus at 10 weeks is not the same as a living baby, and only has the potential to be human. Don't say the foetus is sacred – that kind of language helps no one.

© RE Today Services 2003. Permission is granted to photocopy the cards on this page for use in classroom activities, in schools which have purchased this publication.

Developing Secondary RE: Life, Death and Beyond

Ethics at birth – twenty-five good questions

- Is a human life best described as 'sacred', 'priceless', 'a gift of God' or 'an amazing evolutionary product'?

- What is a foetus? Is 'it' a human, a potential human or is it 'just a cluster of cells'?

- Should the father have a right to veto an abortion, or is it always 'the woman's right to choose'?

- Christians believe God was born on earth to a virgin as Jesus. Doesn't that suggest unusual births can sometimes be part of God's plans?

- Many pregnancies are terminated because of a high risk of a disabled child being born. Does this insult or devalue disabled people? Should we try to end disability through selective termination?

- Soon, science will give us the ability to clone a human. Would this ever be right? Why?

- Does anyone have a 'right' to be a parent? What about children's rights?

- Should couples who have no children be entitled to fertility treatments on the NHS? Is it 'ill health' to be childless?

- In any society where abortion is high, adoption of a new-born baby would be popular with childless couples. Should governments 'fight abortion with adoption'?

- If God is the giver of life, then does that mean humans should never interfere with life? Or should we see ourselves as God's followers, and make loving decisions about birth and death ourselves?

- What is the value of a human life? Where does the value come from?

- Is a human baby more valuable than a baby chimpanzee? Why, or why not?

- Does a child have the right to know who his or her biological parents are? Should anonymous sperm donation be illegal?

- At present the 650 MPs decide the abortion laws. About 500 of them are men. Is it wrong for men to decide what women are allowed to do with their own bodies?

- Is it right for a surrogate mother to 'rent her womb' for 9 months for a couple who can't otherwise have a baby? Would it be wrong to 'rent a womb' just to save a couple 'the bother of pregnancy'?

- If someone has been raped, then is abortion justified because 'it is the lesser of two evils'?

- Some spiritual people say 'life is God's gift'. Do you believe this? What does it mean?

- If using a pig's organs could save a human life, would that be justified (the pig would die)? How should the pig be treated?

- It is possible to 'breed' a younger brother for an older child to be cured of a disease. But is it wrong to make a baby just to get a cure for someone else?

- If parents are allowed to know the gender of their unborn child at conception, might that lead to some parents aborting a girl? Should sexism like that be discouraged by forbidding gender testing on a foetus?

- Is it ever right to end the life of an unborn child? What makes it right or wrong?

- Should abortion be banned after the twentieth week of pregnancy?

- If a couple split up and divorce during a pregnancy, would it be right to allow the woman an abortion for this reason alone?

- When does a life begin? Is it: at conception? As an embryo? When the foetus moves? When the foetus could live outside the womb (about 24 weeks)? At birth?

- Should there be an upper age limit for surrogate parents? Is it fair on a child to be born to a mum in her 60s? 70s? But is it sexist to let men father children up to any age, but deny the freedom to women?

23

Developing Secondary RE: Life, Death and Beyond

Ways to use the twenty-five questions about ethics

Put them onto cards and arrange a 'round table' **discussion**, in which pupils comment on any they find interesting.

Use one question chosen by pupils as a focus for a GCSE RS or Standard Grade practice **essay**.

Categorise: can pupils identify four spiritual questions, four gender questions, four philosophical questions, four medical questions, four legal questions? Are these useful categories? What other categories might be used?

Use a number of the questions as a basis for writing **evaluation** answers in a standard format – a writing frame might ask for three points each 'for and against' and a personal conclusion. Draw pupils' attention to the place of arguments, experiences, commentary on sacred texts and examples in the evaluation process: it's not about expressing prejudice at length!

Ask pupils to **imagine** and **create** situations and characters for a soap opera that explore one of the dilemmas in one of the questions.

Ask pupils in pairs to **choose** one question and complete an '**arguments for and against**' sheet about it, referring to the religions they are studying.

Give pairs of pupils two of the questions and ask them to **write** three paragraphs (100 words each) giving a **viewpoint** from three different perspectives. Choose these from: Roman Catholic Christians; Quaker Christians; Buddhists; Muslims; agnostic humanists; a person who says 'I'm spiritual, but I'm not religious'. Ask learners to include references to their **sources of authority** in their replies.

Use the questions for a **role-play**. The Human Fertilisation and Embryology Authority is a government body for considering these kinds of questions. It contributes to law-making. Select six able pupils from your group to play the part of HFEA members, and ask others in threes to take one of the questions, turn it into a fictional case study or story, and send someone to the HFEA group to ask for a verdict or answer. (See www.hfea.gov.uk)

Ask pupils in pairs to **devise** some more similar questions: twenty-five would be too many, but see if they can raise four more.

24

Developing Secondary RE: Life, Death and Beyond

The sanctity of life – euthanasia

For the teacher

Arguments for and against euthanasia are well rehearsed, but how can the teacher engage pupils in understanding the often subtle and wide-ranging implications of the debate for both individual and society, and the variety of faith perspectives?

How should questions such as the following be addressed?

- **Who should decide** UK law on euthanasia?
- **Is being 'legal' the same as being 'right' and 'good'?** If not, why not?
- **What 'rights' do doctors have?** How might these be protected?
- **Is the law consistent?** Is it consistent to allow suicide, for example, and yet to refuse a person the right to assistance to achieve their death when they are not able to achieve this by themselves (for example, Diane Pretty)?
- **Does the inconsistency of the law frustrate or protect us?** How effectively does it remind us of the complexity of the issues, and keep us mindful of the awesome responsibility we have to preserve life?

See also...

Dutch Voluntary Euthanasia Society
www.nvve.nl/english

UK Voluntary Euthanasia Society (VES)
www.ves.org.uk

BBC Religion and Ethics
www.bbc.co.uk/religion/ethics

Church of England (select 'views on…')
http://cofe.epinet.co.uk

What the Churches Say third edition
(ed. Colin Johnson, CEM, 2000)
www.retoday.org.uk

Euthanasia – a Good Death? (E117)
(Margaret Whipp, Grove Books, 2000)
www.grovebooks.co.uk

What does Islam say? (Ibrahim Hewitt, Muslim Educational Trust, 1998)
www.metpdx.org

Activities for pupils

Activity 1: Diane Pretty and Miss B (page 26)

This activity provides a framework within which pupils can explore the similarities and differences between these two high-profile cases, help explain the different legal judgements, and highlight the wider issues which each case raises. The chart can be enlarged to A4 size.

Pupils could work in pairs to:

a **identify** similarities and differences;

b **identify** three major issues or questions which the cases raise and **feed back** to the class (these could provide a focus for further study);

c **speculate**: if Diane Pretty and Miss B were practising Christians or Muslims, to what extent may their requests have been different?

Activity 2: Dilemmas & Decisions (page 27)

This exercise explores the question: 'If something is legal, does that make it right?'. It is a good way to get pupils to apply what they have learned and to identify questions or areas which need further thought.

There are several ways to 'play' the game – and more examples in *Dilemmas & Decisions* (ed. Lat Blaylock, CEM).

Pupils could:

a **ask a partner** the 'lead question', and follow through the dilemma, according to their response; **reverse roles** and note similarities and differences of response, and speculate on reasons for this;

b **with the whole class, discuss** the implications, and remaining questions raised by the dilemma, **identifying** and **recording** arguments for and against;

c **complete a piece of extended writing**, for example 'How far is it true to say that if something is legal, it is thereby right?' or 'Outline your personal response to the dilemma, making your reasons clear.'

Further activities are outlined on page 28.

25

Developing Secondary RE: Life, Death and Beyond

The right to die ... or ... the right to live?

Diane Pretty

Diane Pretty suffered from motor neurone disease, a distressing, terminal condition which results in death by suffocation. She went to court to get permission to allow her husband to assist her to commit suicide, without fear of his prosecution – that is, she was claiming a positive right to be helped to die. She argued that refusing her would be to violate her rights (under the Human Rights Convention) to life, to protection from inhumane treatment, to privacy and to freedom of thought and belief. Her lawyers argued that a right to life includes a right to die.

Court judgement
A series of courts turned down her request. The judges said that the Convention's aim is to protect life, whereas 'death is the antithesis of life'. It was said at the time: 'If any exception to the 1961 Suicide Act were made, then many vulnerable people would be put at risk.' Euthanasia remains murder and is illegal in the UK. Assisting a suicide is illegal and can result in up to 14 years in prison. **Mrs Pretty died in May 2002.**

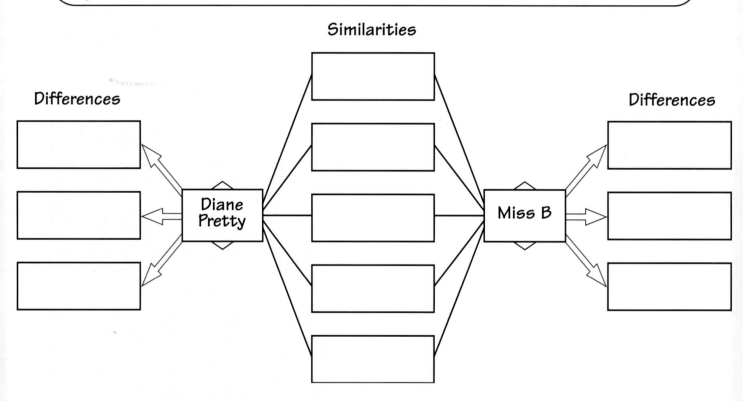

Miss B

Miss B, aged 43, was irreversibly paralysed from the neck down when a blood vessel ruptured in her neck. She was kept alive on a ventilator. Miss B requested that doctors withhold treatment, which they are legally able to do if the request is made by a patient capable of making such a decision. Their intention would not be to kill the patient, but to accept that they couldn't prevent her death. Her doctors refused to grant her request as it went against their ethical principles of seeking to preserve life, and so the case went to court.

Miss B claimed a negative right not to be treated against her will.

Court judgement
In April 2002 a High Court judge gave Miss B permission to refuse further treatment. She said that Miss B had 'the necessary mental capacity to give consent or refuse consent to life-sustaining medical treatment.' **Miss B died in May 2002, when medical staff turned off her ventilator at her request.**

© RE Today Services 2003. Permission is granted to photocopy this page for use in classroom activities, in schools which have purchased this publication.

Developing Secondary RE: Life, Death and Beyond

Dilemmas & Decisions ... does being legal make something right?

You are a journalist and have just begun researching a series of articles on euthanasia, prompted by the recent death of your maternal grandfather in a local hospice. You are uncertain of your own views about euthanasia and would describe your outlook on life as humanist.

A colleague tells you that she has a contact you may wish to interview – Hannah, a 45-year-old Dutch woman in the final stages of cancer who has made arrangements for her euthanasia in 5 days' time. Hannah is a member of the Dutch Reformed (Protestant) Church, and despite controversy over the changes in the euthanasia law, some members of her church are supporting her. Hannah has said she is willing to be interviewed by a sympathetic journalist, and wants to be as open and honest as she can about death, dying and euthanasia. This is a unique opportunity for you. **Do you agree to do the interview?**

YES

You travel to Holland, and meet Hannah at her home. She is an intelligent and well-educated woman who has travelled widely; you get on well together from the start. Hannah never married and is now approaching death with the support of some members of her church. After much conversation over 2 days, Hannah asks if you will accompany her to the place she has chosen for her euthanasia. She is happy to continue to talk with you, and for you to record her thoughts, until the doctor arrives. You could then leave. **Do you agree?**

YES (NO: question ends)

You continue your conversation with Hannah. She talks more now about her faith in God, the struggles she has had with her conscience as she considered euthanasia, and how her church friends have supported her, even when not all agreed with her decision. The doctor arrives. Hannah has explained to you what will happen and now asks if you will stay with her at this final and most intimate of times. **Do you agree to stay with Hannah until she dies?**

NO

Your mother is diagnosed with cancer and is given 3 months to live. She has read about the new law which came into effect on 1 April 2002 in Holland, and knows that you had the opportunity to interview Hannah. Your mother asks you to find out about the procedure for visitors to Holland to be given euthanasia. You know that Hannah is someone who can give you all the information and insights you need. **Do you now agree to interview Hannah?**

NO (YES: question ends)

You explain your reasons to your mother, and she becomes distressed. You tell her about the local hospice, and how doctors there can help ensure that she is in as little pain and discomfort as possible, but she insists she doesn't want to die like her father did, and that she wants to know about Holland. She is too ill to find the information for herself, and doesn't want to upset other members of the family. **Do you now agree to interview Hannah?**

Developing Secondary RE: Life, Death and Beyond

Reflecting and responding

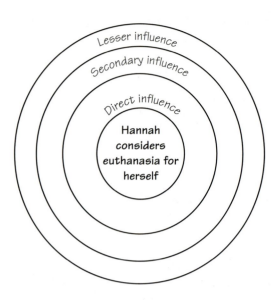

Activity 1 – Considering influences

a **Identify** the factors that might have influenced Hannah's decision for voluntary euthanasia. **Decide** whether each factor is a **direct**, **secondary** or **lesser** influence.

b **Complete** an 'influences' diagram (see example) for:
- Hannah;
- yourself;
- a Muslim (if you are a Muslim, draw a diagram for an atheist).

Note: Draw or write a word or other symbol for each factor you identify in the appropriate circuit of the diagram.

c **Discuss** any similarities and differences between the three records. What do you think explains them?

Activity 2 – Considering similarities and differences

Use a copy of the similarities and differences chart on page 26 to compare what the following groups say about **euthanasia** on their **websites**:

- **Roman Catholic Church** (http://217.19.224.165) and **Church of England** (http://cofe.epinet.co.uk);
- **Church of England** (http://cofe.epinet.co.uk) and **British Humanist Association** (www.humanism.org.uk);
- **Islam** (www.islamicmedicine.org/views.htm) and **Roman Catholic Church** (http://217.19.224.165).

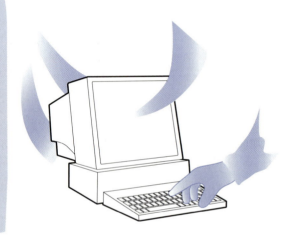

Activity 3 – Extended writing

a) The journalist
Imagine you are the journalist and that you are writing up your interview with Hannah. You intend to send it to her church. **Compose** the opening and closing paragraphs.

b) Conversation
Compose the conversation the journalist had with Hannah about life, death, dying and belief in God.

c) Visitor to an RE lesson
Imagine the journalist is asked to speak to a class of 15-year-old pupils in a local high school as part of their GCSE Religious Studies course. **Plan** what she says.

Activity 4 – Dilemmas & Decisions

Develop a 'Dilemmas & Decisions' exercise of your own following these guidelines:

a **Choose** a topic you have studied, and **devise** an introductory statement using the second person singular. End with a question which requires a 'Yes' or 'No' answer.

b **Devise** two 'Yes' statements, ending with a question. Each time it must be harder to answer 'Yes'.

c **Devise** two 'No' statements, ending with a question. Each time it must be harder to answer 'No'.

d **Try it out** with another group, and **revise** it in the light of any suggestions made!

Developing Secondary RE: Life, Death and Beyond

Responding to issues in medical ethics

For the teacher

Many Agreed Syllabuses and GCSE specifications require various aspects of medical ethics to be studied, and from a variety of faith standpoints. These issues are complex, with new information, applications and responses appearing almost daily.

The activities included in this section aim to be **adaptable** and **flexible**, and provide opportunities for pupils of all abilities to apply and reflect on their learning.

The **websites** given on this page will provide a useful reference point for the latest information and debate.

See also...

Gattaca (1997)
This film explores a 'brave new world' of the future where only 'valid' genetically engineered people have significance. **Extracts** can provide useful stimulus to discussion.

RS Web
RS gateway site supporting GCE and GCSE RS. www.rsweb.org.uk

BBC's Gene Stories
An interactive and informative introduction to a range of issues. www.bbc.co.uk/genes

CMF (Christian Medical Fellowship)
A vast range of articles on medical and other ethical issues offering well-informed Christian perspectives. www.cmf.org.uk

Ethics for Schools
A resource for schools from CMF (see above) linked to all major GCSE and GCE exam boards for RS. www.ethicsforschools.org

Ethics Updates
This USA site provides updates and discussion forums for most issues in ethics for teachers and pupils. http://ethics.acusd.edu

Human Genome Project
Extensive site funded by the USA government to provide information on the Project. www.ornl.gov/hgmis

Activity 1 – Story-start

The story-start on page 30 is based on a **true story**, and its use is **flexible**. It can support:

- individual or small group work;
- classwork or homework;
- extended writing or drama presentation.

In the version presented here, the wife of the main character is a Roman Catholic Christian. This introduces a focus for religious perspectives to be explored by pupils, a detail which can be varied to suit syllabus requirements. This is the only detail not found in the original storyline.

The story format gives pupils a chance to:

→ **try out** some points of view;
→ **express** their own ideas;
→ **plot their way** through a situation so that they **consider** what this aspect of medical ethics might mean to different people and to themselves.

Activity 2 – Role-play

This resource (pages 31–32) provides opportunity for a whole class to **apply** what they have learned and **reflect** on the process of decision-making.

a **Allocate** roles either at random or by discretion; cards can be adapted to suit other topics (e.g. euthanasia) and religious perspectives.

b **Photocopy** all the panel member cards and sufficient role cards for all members of the class, ensuring a fair spread of type of role cards.

c **Provide** pupils with sufficient preparation time. Also ensure all understand the nature of the activity, how they should respond and contribute, and the follow-up work required (see page 31).

d Arrange the room so that the panel members face the rest of the group and hold the meeting. A time limit should be set for this (e.g. 20 minutes).

e Debrief and complete the written task.

Developing Secondary RE: Life, Death and Beyond

Glimpsing the future ... enhancing the present?

In June 2000 'The Human Genome Project' produced a working draft of the entire human genome sequence (see: www.ornl.gov/hgmis). One of many **possibilities** following this research is DNA-based testing. Genetic tests can be used for a variety of reasons, including estimating the risk of developing cancers and Alzheimer's disease. The **benefits** and **concerns** of such testing are highlighted in the following true story.

Activity for pupils

a **Read** the passage below, which describes what happened to David Duncan when he decided to take advantage of what the new tests seemed to offer.

b **Decide** what happens next – and **complete** the story in your own words (350 words maximum).

c **For reflection:** What decision might you have made in David's situation?

This is how it all began ...

I am a 44-year-old family man, and a science writer. I have followed the progress of the Human Genome Project with enthusiasm, and have just written a book about the technology of screening genes.

As I finished the book I asked myself: **'What if I had myself screened for any defect it was possible to detect?'**

Before going ahead I talked it over with my family – my wife, who is a **Roman Catholic Christian**, and our three children, aged 15, 13 and 7. What if I am carrying the gene for Alzheimer's, Huntington's, a cancer or heart disease? **My genetic future could also be theirs.**

I went for counselling to help me cope with the outcome, whatever it might be. Did I know that the tests only give a 'probability' for developing the disorder? Was I aware of the difficulty of interpreting a positive result as some people who carry a disease-associated mutation never develop the disease? And what about the chance of laboratory error...? **So many questions.**

I persuaded a well-known biotechnology company to conduct the test – a swab taken from inside the cheek. This was the easy part!

I wondered if I had done the right thing. I had entered the room healthy and happy – would the results leave me in despair?

I felt naked. Exposed. As if my skin, bone, muscle tissue, cells had all been peeled back, down to a tidy swirl of DNA.

I watched the results pop up on a computer screen, and was guided through them.

Negative for a gene that can cause liver damage. **Clear** of a variation linked to lung cancer. Free of a gene mutation associated with a condition where the blood retains too much iron.

Then a line of results on the monitor turned red and the initials MT flashed up: I had a mutant type. **I felt the blood drain from my face...**

Based on an article by Sarah Baxter and Jonathan Leake in the Sunday Times *13 October 2002. Published with permission.*

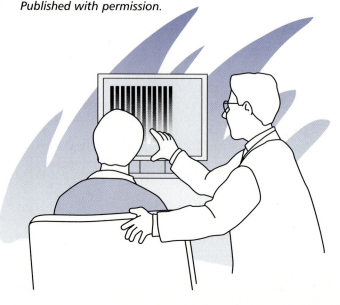

Developing Secondary RE: *Life, Death and Beyond*

You the jury – should the cloning of human beings be allowed?

Background
The UK government is reviewing the law relating to the cloning of humans. Current law allows only the cloning of stem cells (therapeutic cloning).

Government officials are keen to learn the views of as wide a range of people as possible before a decision is made.

You are invited to a local meeting at which the issue will be debated. At the end of the meeting a vote will be taken, and a report of the proceedings sent to the government.

Written work
Following the role-play, each member of the group will compose a statement (250 words) which expresses 'best advice' (in role) to the government.

Instructions
Study the details on your role card. You have 15 minutes to prepare for your role.

→ **The chairperson** prepares a 60-second introduction to the purpose of the meeting.

→ **Panel members** prepare a 60-second introductory statement reflecting the views of members of the group they represent (setting the scene and raising key questions).

→ **Role-players** familiarise themselves with the religious or ethical views of the person they represent, and prepare three questions which that person would want to have answered before making a decision.

When everyone is prepared, the meeting is held, and a vote taken. **Should the UK government change the current law to allow the cloning of human beings?**

Chairperson
As chairperson, you introduce the context of the meeting, ensure that everyone contributes to the discussion and that an outcome is arrived at and reported fairly. You must be objective; your personal religious, political and ethical views should remain private during the meeting.

Panel member 1 — Christian
You are the leader of the local Christian ecumenical group. This consists of representatives of Roman Catholic, Anglican (Church of England) and free churches (for example, Methodists, Salvation Army and Quakers). You represent a variety of views on cloning.

Panel member 2 — Muslim
You are a Muslim, and a member of your local mosque. You have three children, one of whom is adopted. Your spouse is a doctor in the gynaecology department of the local hospital.

Panel member 3 — Humanist
5 years ago you joined the British Humanist Association, and shortly afterwards began working for them full time. You regularly represent the BHA in, for example, TV interviews and magazine articles, and visit schools to lead RE lessons and assemblies.

Role card 1 — Christian
You have been married for 20 years and have three children. Your spouse has recently been diagnosed with motor neurone disease, a progressive illness which cannot be cured.

Role card 2 — Agnostic
You have just completed a 2-week work experience placement with a major adoption charity. You met several young men and women seeking to trace their birth mother and have become aware of how crucial this is to many adopted children.

Developing Secondary RE: Life, Death and Beyond

Role card 3 — Humanist
You are an identical twin. Although physically identical, you are distinct and healthy individuals in all other respects. Some scientists say you and your twin have more in common than Dolly the sheep and her mother.

Role card 4 — Christian
You are a doctor at the local hospital. One of your patients has just died because an organ transplant was not available in time. The acute shortage of healthy donated organs for transplant is a great concern to you.

Role card 5 — Christian
You visit your elderly grandmother most days on your way home from school. She has just been diagnosed with Alzheimer's, for which there is currently no cure.

Role card 6 — Muslim
You are a writer and broadcaster on a range of ethical issues. Your latest programme has explored how cloning a human might affect inter-human relationships (for example, between parent and child, sibling and child, extended family and child).

Role card 7 — Muslim
You are a research scientist. You were a member of the team which worked with Professor Ian Wilmot and produced the cloned sheep known as 'Dolly'.

Role card 8 — Muslim
You are a psychologist and deal regularly with people confused about their identity; some were adopted as babies and know nothing of their birth parents. You wonder if a cloned human would show similar psychological distress.

Role card 9 — Christian
Your elder brother, aged 45, has just been diagnosed with Parkinson's disease. He is married with two children at university, and a third child in Year 10 at the local high school. He is the headteacher of a primary school. You are the minister of a local church.

Role card 10 — Muslim
You are the imam of the local mosque. You and your wife have been trying for a family for several years with no success. You have considered IVF treatment, and also whether cloning technology might help, but are worried about what your Muslim friends might say should you take action.

Role card 11 — Christian
You are a member of the Guild of Catholic Doctors, which holds that the life of the human embryo has special status and should be protected in all circumstances. You are married with two children under 16.

Role card 12 — Humanist
You are a laboratory technician. For the last 4 years you have worked for an Italian professor who claims that he will shortly be able to clone babies for infertile couples.

Role card 13 — Muslim
You are a doctor in a busy local health centre. From time to time you have patients who are unable to conceive, and ask for help. At the moment you can only suggest IVF treatment, which is expensive and has a low success rate.

Role card 14 — Agnostic
You are a teacher at the local high school. Members of your tutor group have been talking with you about their work on genetic engineering and cloning in RE, and have asked you to raise a variety of questions at the meeting on their behalf.